MW00325575

Eve's Choice

BONNIE J. ARMANTROUT

LifeRich Publishing is a registered trademark of The Reader's Digest Association, Inc.

LifeRich Publishing books may be ordered through booksellers or by contacting:

LifeRich Publishing
1663 Liberty Drive
Bloomington, IN 47403
www.liferichpublishing.com
844-686-9607

scriptures taken from NKJV

ISBN: 978-1-4897-3626-0 (sc)
ISBN: 978-1-4897-3624-6 (hc)
ISBN: 978-1-4897-3625-3 (e)

Library of Congress Control Number: 2021910908

Print information available on the last page.

LifeRich Publishing rev. date: 06/02/2021

Dedication

Eve's Choice is dedicated to young people everywhere making their decision for Christ. Young people are learning, as Eve learned, that behavior is a reflection of life's choices. Living life for self or living life for God is a personal choice.

Like Eve's choice for fruit, we learn that our choices for obedience are the fruit of our love for God (John 3:16).

Contents

Our Characters Are...

God: Together with His Son, Creator of everything by His spoken word. He is the Ancient of Days.

God always has been and always will be. For God so loved the world.

Christ: Together with His Father, Christ is Creator of everything by His spoken word. The Lord Jesus Christ, Michael, God's Son, Lamb of God, Lamb who was slain, Son of Man, Redeemer of the world, Lord of Lords, and King of Kings. He is the Alpha and Omega, Beginning and the End, the First and the Last. He is who is and who was and who is to come. He is the Almighty, King of saints, the Faithful Witness, the First Born from the dead, the Ruler over the kings of the earth. I am who I am. Jesus the Christ, Jesus, the Root and offspring of David. He is the Bright and Morning Star and Mary's Son. I am He who lives and was dead. I am alive forever more (Genesis 1–3).

Adam: Created from the dust of the earth. Adam was Eve's husband, father of all living, the first man. Adam and Eve were the caretakers of the Garden of Eden.

Eve: Created by God from the rib of Adam. Eve was Adam's wife, mother of all living, and the first woman.

Gabriel: An angel who stands in the presence of God. An angel who made announcements down through time to Daniel, Mary, and John the Baptist.

Lucifer: Known as Satan, the lawless one, the devil, the serpent, the prince of the air, and the dragon (Revelation 12:7–9).

1

Gabriel Remembers

You are caught in the moment. You see bright hues of color everywhere. You see brilliant yellow sunshine wrapping itself around nature's many forms. You see trees that reach past the forest's lush lower growth. The full low-lying ferns are showing off their sprays of green. They stretch, arching broad and gentle. They bend low, bringing you down to the rich, moist soil. Flower blossoms are nodding their heavy pastel heads, gently bouncing and reaching for the sun.

Listen. There is a collection of nature's sounds. You hear the breeze gently tossing the leaves as they hurry along their way. The brook is babbling, as if off to a grand destination. It is running, winding in its own independent course through the rocks and soil. Birds are singing loudly, each singing its own song of cheer. *Chee, chee, chee* is their loud announcement, proclaiming a new day has come.

Take in the moment you are revering. Realize where you are; it is a holy place. It is awesome, much different from any other place. Everything seems brighter, more focused. Everything is grand and imbued with wonder. You are at the entrance of the garden of God, the Garden of Eden.

Shading your eyes from the brightness, you strain to focus. Through the brilliant light you see forms and a structure in the distance. There are enormous gates and ribbon-like walls. The gates are overwhelming. Their massive structure and brilliance fade into the sky. As you move closer, you see they are the entrance to the Garden of Eden. The brilliant forms are angels guarding Eden's entrance. The angels are glowing almost white. The space encircling their forms shares the same glow. As you approach you see two angels standing on either side of the gates. They are commanding at their posts.

The angels hold themselves very still, statue-like. They exude honor, strength, and respect. Rays of light bend and stretch away from them. The swords of the celestial guard share the brilliance of their wings.

To the side of the garden gate is a third angel. He is not as commanding but is still very grand. He seems more personable, more approachable. This is Gabriel. He is standing by himself and waiting. He intently remembers his charge, his command, his service. He remembers Eve's request and waits.

2

Eve Talks to Gabriel

Gabriel, standing to the side of the gates, is remembering a time when Eve wandered back to God's garden gates to visit, to be part of what her world used to be. To find the comfort, the home she had once had.

Eve approached the garden gates and followed the path that bordered the massive garden walls. Although she had started out wandering without a destination, in her heart she knew she needed to go to the garden gates. From there, she and Gabriel would talk and walk. They would walk along the outer edge of the walls of the Garden of Eden as they had done so many times before. Gabriel gave Eve long-sought comfort and hope, comfort and hope that faded when she was away from the garden gates and the glory that shone from them.

3

Scorn of the Family

Away from the garden gates were many gatherings of Eve's people. They were Eve's family, generations of her children. Eve was the first mother. She was the mother of all living people.

Some members of the family used to be followers of God, but now they only scoffed and ridiculed Eve. The family now chose not to visit the garden gates. They thought Eve and Adam, her husband, were the reasons the leaves died and no one could now go through the garden gates to enter the Garden of Eden. The family felt Adam and Eve had brought all their hardships upon them. The family's hardness of heart grew until most didn't believe in God at all. Eve needed her people, her family. But to see them and know that they didn't know what it was like to walk and talk with God was almost more than she could bear.

So Eve, needing assurance, would wander to the garden gates in search of Gabriel to feel the glory of God and the assurance of salvation. Her life was without Adam now. Adam had died, and she was alone. Away from the gates, Eve's hope would fade. She would search her mind and wonder whether the sacrifice of the Lamb would be enough. Would her sins be forgiven (Hebrews 9:11; Revelation 5)?

Time after time Gabriel and Eve talked and walked together. Eve enjoyed reliving when she and Adam lived in the garden together, when she and Adam would walk and talk, not with Gabriel but directly with God. Eve was remembering life in the garden of God. Remembering before Adam had died, before she had found the tree.

4

Eve and the Serpent

Eve had been gathering fruit in the garden. She carefully selected what she thought was the best fruit for Adam. She thought, *Adam will enjoy this fruit so much!* She could see the fruit's rich color. She could smell its ripeness. Why hadn't she noticed the fruit before? She was so excited about her new find that she quickened her pace. She cradled the fruit in her arms, carefully balancing each piece.

A snake, a most beautiful animal, flew by and gently landed on a tree near Eve. She saw the snake in flight and his brilliant form as she had many times before. But this time Eve was startled. The snake was talking—and to her! Eve wondered why none of the other snakes had spoken to her. *Why,* she wondered, *did he speak at all?*

This snake seemed so wise. He told Eve of her own amazing beauty. The snake saw her pausing in thought, wondering about him. The snake quickly explained,

"Only a few of the animals in the garden can speak." He was surprised she didn't know of them. After all, she and Adam cared for each of the animals. In fact, God gave him the responsibility to name them all.

The snake talked as he ate of the fruit of the tree. He told Eve that it was, "most delicious!" After the snake had a few bites of the fruit, he offered it to Eve, explaining that if she just held his fruit, she would see it was quite harmless. Actually, it would give her new wisdom. She could see he had wisdom. After all, he was an animal, and he could talk. He told her she had already been gathering fruit beside his tree, and she could see it was harmless.

Eve's mind repeated the words, *Harmless. Harmless? Why would such a lovely fruit be considered harmful? Why was this fruit so tempting?* When her racing mind settled, she realized this was the Tree of the Knowledge of Good and Evil. Touching this tree—let alone eating its fruit—would directly disobey God.

5

Eve's Choice

This was the tree that God had said not to touch or eat from. If they did, Adam and Eve would surely die. But there she was, balancing an armful of fruit from a tree directly beside that forbidden tree. Now the snake had suggested the fruit of his tree was harmless. Eve's eyes and the snake's eyes met. She paused as if to look at the snake for reassurance.

6

Wisdom

"It's OK, Eve," the snake said. "You saw me eat it, and you see I am more wise and beautiful than all the other animals. God knows the plan. He knows when you eat the fruit you will rise to higher knowledge and new wisdom. I am an animal, and you see how much wiser I am after eating the fruit.

"I am beautiful. I can reason with you, and I can speak. Can you imagine what wisdom and powers you will have as a human being? Just imagine touching the fruit, Eve. Imagine holding it and feeling the wisdom."

Eve was locked in attention. She let the snake, the great serpent, talk her through imagining holding a piece of fruit as it hung from the branch. Eve imagined the softness, the tenderness, the weight of the fruit in her hand.

"It will be OK, Eve. I am here with you. I wouldn't let anything happen to you. Just one bite."

So Eve took a bite of the fruit of the serpent's tree. "See, Eve, you are not struck dead as was promised you. You now have more wisdom than before."

Eve had to admit the fruit did taste good; she savored the taste. She had not tasted anything like it in all the garden. Out of habit, she quickly turned to tell Adam, to share with him her new find. At that moment Eve wondered, *Where is Adam?* She realized she hadn't seen him for a while. Her mind racing, her eyes searching, she became aware she had wandered from Adam.

Eve had chosen to parley with the snake, the serpent. She had been at the forbidden Tree of Knowledge of Good and Evil. Eve had eaten of its fruit. Eve had had a choice to believe and obey her God, to resist the temptation of the forbidden fruit. But looking to the beautiful snake, she had held the fruit. A position of compromise between Eve and the serpent had led to "Just one bite." Eve had eaten the forbidden fruit! She had made her choice.

The fruit now tasted bitter. She spit it out over and over. Eve had made a choice that changed the course many down through time would travel. Her choice to dishonor her Creator was done. She chosen the serpent as her master by her behavior. *Oh,* she thought frantically, *where is Adam?* How long had they been separated from each other? Overcome with fear, Eve frantically rushed through the garden, searching for and calling Adam.

She soon found him as he, in turn, was looking for her. Eve was distraught, shaken. Adam listened to her explain her search for select fruit for him. He listened to her tell of the beautiful, flying, talking snake. She hadn't wanted to disobey. Adam understood she had made her choice, Eve's choice. Her disobedience expressed her lack of faith in God. She hadn't wanted to disobey, but after wandering away from Adam, she was tempted by the one that God and the angels had warned them about. They had been warned about Satan, who was the serpent, the dragon, Lucifer, and the great deceiver.

Adam now depended on himself versus God, his loving Master. He had to decide if he would forever lose his beloved wife, who was a part of his flesh, or choose to trust God. The thought terrified him. He could not bear the idea of being separated from Eve. She had sinned, but he had felt terribly alone while he looked for Eve. How could he bear to be without her forever? Adam quickly grabbed the fruit and ate it too. He too made his choice. He loved Eve, and he could not stand the thought of being without her for a moment. So Eve's choice influenced Adam's choice to disobey. Adam chose based on his own wisdom.

7

Banished from the Garden of God

The garden now seemed more still. The air was cool. As Adam and Eve quickly moved about, they could hear God walking in the garden (Genesis 3:8). Fearful, they could hear God calling their names. They hid from God, hoping to delay their confrontation, hoping to find some way to explain their choices to disobey, their choice to distrust God. Eve had distrusted God when she trusted that the serpent would take care of her. Adam had distrusted God because he was fearful of life without Eve.

The prince of the air, Satan, the serpent had used the snake to impress Eve. Now Satan, through the snake, was Adam and Eve's god. He had dominion over the earth, Adam, and Eve. Adam and Eve knew the serpent was right. Their wisdom had increased. They not only had knowledge of good but also of evil. They were ashamed and afraid.

God found them and shared their deep sorrow. He explained they would be kept from the Tree of Life to prevent eternal sin and disobedience. God shared how the world would slowly die to lawlessness (John 3:4). Not that day, but over time they too would die. But before then, they would have to leave their garden home, which was where the Tree of Life stood. God shared that yes, they now had new wisdom, knowledge of good and knowledge of evil. But their beautiful Garden of Eden home, the garden of God, would no longer be their home.

The angels quietly came and showed Adam and Eve the entrance to the gated garden. The grandiose garden gates and walls enclosed the garden, and the gates were its only entrance. The angels led them out of the garden reminding them not to return. Slowly, the realization of angelic instruction became more than real to the unholy pair. They were banned forever from their garden home. As they quickly turned back toward the entrance, they saw the swords of the angels, swords held high and gleaming in the sun. The two angels were guarding over the garden of God.

Angels kept their watch at the garden gates. Their commanding presence affirmed their mission as watchmen. Their drawn swords, long and straight, glistened in the sun, joining the rays shining from the angels. God had gently explained to Adam and Eve the new wisdom that made them unable to stay in their Eden home. God would no longer walk and talk with them.

But although not always seen, their guardian angel, Gabriel, was always with them. Gabriel would walk and talk, reassure them, and further explain their new wisdom, the plan of salvation. Because of God's love for them, Christ, God's Son, would make atonement, ransom them. He would be their substitute in death, a Redeemer. Christ would be the victor over the serpent, Satan (Hebrews 2:14).

The sacrifice of a lamb would substitute for Christ, God's Son (Leviticus 4:32), until a man-child would be born of a woman and die on a tree, the cross. Christ's blood would repay the ransom of humankind. God loved them and hadn't left them comfortless. Attempting to reassure Eve, time after time, Adam repeated the plan of salvation to her.

Eve's confidence was shaken, her self-condemnation overpowering, the heaviness of her thoughts overwhelming. She didn't know how she would take another breath. How she could live with her thoughts of how she had dishonored God. Adam repeatedly reminded Eve that Christ, God's Son, would pay the penalty of death. Death and sin were their new wisdom. They would sacrifice a lamb, a symbol of salvation of Christ's blood until Christ would come. Although Adam reassured Eve, in his heart he too needed courage that the plan of salvation was enough. He needed to verbalize their choice to believe that salvation's plan was enough. He too needed the courage that the plan of salvation gave them both.

They knelt morning and evening at the gates of the garden of God, obeying their Creator and praying for His guidance and protection. It was a physical display of their faith, and their faith was their hope in Christ, their Redeemer. They prayed that Eve would have a man-child to be the Savior of their choice.

8

Death at the Gates

Eve separated from the family gatherings to visit the garden gates. She separated to feel the warm hope that the gates provided. Gabriel and Eve were walking outside the garden walls. Adam had died. She was without Adam now, alone. When Adam died, Gabriel had comforted her in her grief, reminding her of the plan of salvation. Gabriel helped her as she laid Adam in his grave. She covered Adam with a mixture of the moist dark soil and her tears, as she and Adam together had laid their son, Abel. Adam wanted to be laid close to the garden gates for when God would call him. "When the dead in Christ would rise at the sound of the trumpet" (1 Corinthians 15:52).

So Adam was in his grave sleeping the sleep of death, waiting for God's call.

9

Witness of the Leaf

Gabriel and Eve circled the garden walls. Eve began to pick up fallen leaves from the ground. Big leaves, little leaves, leaves from all kinds of trees had fallen. It was then Eve also remembered Adam when, in all his horror, was on his knees rocking back and forth. He held his collection of leaves in his arms, picking them up from the ground. He was cradling as many leaves as his arms could hold. Adam was picking up leaves that would again fall, spilling out of his arms. Eve immediately knew she was the cause of his distress. Adam and Eve had been the caretakers, the stewards of nature. Adam had named the animals, and together they had trained the vines of the garden. Adam's distress was because of her. The leaves were dying, falling from the trees to the ground, and it was her fault. Death was her fault. It had been her choice. Adam's grief was her fault. What had she done? She had caused the knowledge of sin, death to be part of the world.

How many throughout time would suffer for her choice of choosing another god, Satan, Lucifer. Eve remembered bending over, holding onto Adam as his bent form swayed back and forth. Adam was swaying, crying, and clutching his fallen leaves. His beautiful leaves were dying. It had been the first sign of death for the unholy pair, the first sign of the serpent's new wisdom.

10

So Adam and Eve had waited for the birth of the first
man-child to save them, to redeem them from Eve's
choice. Many generations later, still no Redeemer. But
they had hope, faith, and obedience to comfort them.
Each time they obeyed God, it strengthened their faith.
In His love, God gave them knowledge of obedience and
faith to strengthen them.

Not all family members clung to their hope but moved
from sorrow to despair to hate for Adam and Eve. Family
stopped visiting the garden gates. Their hope faded, and
their anger grew. The family's behavior was a display of
their choice. It was a display of their choice in Satan, the
prince of the air.

11

In Pursuit of Assurance

Gabriel had explained the plan of salvation to Adam and Eve over and over. Now Gabriel explained it to just Eve. She felt so alone. She returned again and again to the garden gates to be close to where Adam was buried. Being close to the garden gates offered her the hope of salvation.

Gabriel had again found her at the gates, overcome with grief. Eve needed the touch of faith. She needed to feel the warm glory of the hope of God shining on her. So she tarried at the gates. The family gatherings didn't bring the same hope she had shared with Adam. They didn't obey God or teach their children to obey God. They had no faith that a Redeemer would come. Eve had told her children's children the story of Eden, hoping they would understand and share in the hope of salvation with her.

12

Redemption Was Enough

Although Eve had memories of Eden's story and the plan of salvation, she needed repeated reassurance. Her fears and doubts wore away at her hope until once again she needed to feel the glory of the garden gates. Then she would return to sit by Adam's grave by the light of the gates. The light that shone from the angels told of the glory of God. It was the light that made her hope of a Redeemer most real to her. It was being there that made her choice to believe in salvation real to her. Again overcome with grief, Eve asked Gabriel for reassurance that redemption was enough. She asked Gabriel to again tell her the story of salvation, this time at the garden gates. Eve asked to know more than she had before. She needed Gabriel's assurance that salvation would be certain.

13

Panorama of Events

Gabriel began to explain as Eve had asked so many times before. He explained Lucifer's desire to be God, Lucifer's choice, and his fall from heaven. How by their choice, Lucifer took one third of the angels with him from heaven before the creation of the earth. (2 Thessalonians 2:9; Revelation 12:4).

Lucifer had been banned from heaven and wanted to be God. But God had a plan for man's salvation. He again explained redemption through the blood of the Lamb. Adam and Eve would sacrifice a lamb as a symbol of Christ's blood. One day the man-child, Christ, would shed His blood, the ransom for humankind. Christ's death was the complete sacrifice for humankind. How through Adam and Eve's choice of faith and obedience to God they would again walk and talk with God in the garden. The family gatherings would also walk and talk with God if they made their choice through faith to obey God.

Gabriel revealed to Eve a visual panorama of world events to come. He showed Eve forward through the halls of providence of time that there were those who would have a right to the Tree of Life. He explained to Eve the generations of decisions to be made for Christ. Decisions for Christ made because Eve chose faith in the redemption through the plan of salvation (Revelation 22:14).

Times yet to come would ebb and flow as Satan wanted to claim his stake as the prince of the air. Eve's choice, man's choice for God would carry the victory at the cross. Christ the Redeemer would come and pay the blood ransom for all humankind.

14

Eve's Request

As they walked, Gabriel became aware that Eve was much calmer. Her form was more assured and her steps more confident. Nature's evening sounds quieted as the sun settled its evening light. Gabriel and Eve walked toward the garden gates. Gabriel asked Eve if she had any other needs before she returned to her family. She paused and slowly turned to Gabriel. Eve explained to Gabriel she was aware that she too would lie down and not rise again, as Adam had done. She would sleep the sleep of death. But when this time came, she did not want to wait alone for God to call her. She knew God had provided her angel Gabriel to comfort her. Eve quietly but plainly asked Gabriel if after she died, after she fell into the sleep of death waiting for God, if he would wait by her grave till the trumpet of God called her, called her from her grave by the gates of the garden.

15

Gabriel Waits

At the end of the evening, Eve did not return to any of the family gatherings. Eve choose to pause and nap in the long, lush ferns. She was refreshed and assured with the hope of salvation. She enjoyed the smell of the moist green ferns as she drifted off to sleep. Eve slept as Gabriel waited by her sleeping form. He waited till the rise of the sun, which shone so brilliant. Its rays were bright and warm. Gabriel waited until the morning sun reflected strong off the glowing swords of the celestial guards. Gabriel waited till the running, babbling brook, the singing birds, and the nodding flowers were all honoring their Creator in the morning sun. Gabriel waited at his post with his charge Eve as she lay asleep.

16

Gabriel Remembers

Gabriel was finishing his labor. Kneeling, he felt the moist, dark earth fall between his fingers. He was returning the dark soil. He felt the moist earth between his fingers as Eve's hair had done as he laid her in her grave. Her sleep of death now began till she and Adam would both hear God's trumpet call together.

Gabriel waited by Eve's burial place at the gates. Gabriel was remembering Eve's choice of redemption. Valiant courage of obedience through faith in God's plan of salvation was Eve's hope. Her choice was to receive and be a part of God's faith. Obedience was the evidence of her choice. Quietly, Gabriel waited, intently remembering his charge Eve and waiting for God's call of the trumpet by the garden gate. It is a holy place, much different from any other.

17

Providence: A Place for You and Me

Providence, God's love, foresight, and protection has supplied you and me a place, a holy place much different from any other. A place where in our hearts, our hope is in the coming of the Lord. It is a place where we are the fruits of Christ's creation. Providence is a place where we, too, have the right to the Tree of Life and may enter through the gates into the city.